THE BASICS OF
WINNING
VIDEO
POKER

J. Edward Allen

- Gambling Research Institute -
Cardoza Publishing

Cardoza Publishing, publisher of Gambling Research Institute (GRI) books, is the foremost gaming and gambling publisher in the world with a library of more than 75 up-to-date and easy-to-read books and strategies. These authoritative works are written by the top experts in their fields and with more than 5,000,000 books in print, represent the best-selling and most popular gaming books anywhere.

PRINTING HISTORY

First Printing	*September 1990*
2nd Edition	
First Printing	*January 1993*
Second Printing	*August 1993*
Third Printing	*March 1995*
3rd Edition	
First Printing	*January 1998*

ISBN:0-940685-97-3
Library of Congress Catalogue Card Number: 97-94819

Special thanks to International Game Technology for permission to use front cover photo.

CARDOZA PUBLISHING

P.O. Box 1500, Cooper Station, New York, NY 10276
Phone (718)743-5229 • Fax (718) 743-8284
E-Mail: cardozapub@aol.com

Table of Contents

Tables and Charts

I. Introduction

Video poker can be beaten! Decision-making and skill is involved, and in this book, we'll show you how to make the proper plays and be a winner!

Many people think they're the same as slot machines, but there's a big difference. With slots, there's no decision making process, while at video poker you have to make correct plays to win.

Having skill at this game pays off, especially when there are jackpots involved. The payoffs can be lucrative, running into the thousands of dollars. And the game can be beaten even without hitting the big payoffs for it's structured so that, assuming best play by the gambler, it is practically an even-up game with the casino!

In this book, we're going to introduce you to the fascinating world of computerized video poker, showing the various machines you can play, how to play them correctly, and how to be a winner at this game!

II. How to Play Video Poker

Introduction to Poker Hands

For those of you who don't understand poker but want to play video poker, we'll briefly show the varying kinds of hands in descending order of strength, with the best hand listed first.

Chart 1: Poker Hands

Royal Flush - A K Q J 10 of the same suit.

Straight Flush - Any five card sequence in the same suit, such as J 10 9 8 7. Also A 2 3 4 5.

Four of a Kind - All four cards of the same value such as 7 7 7 7.

Full House - Three of a kind combined with a pair, such as 4 4 4 Q Q.

Flush - Any five cards of the same suit, but not in sequence.

Straight - Five cards in sequence, but not in the same suit, such as Q J 10 9 8. Also A 2 3 4 5.

Three of a Kind - Three cards of the same rank, such as 10 10 10.

Two Pair - Two separate pairs such as 8 8 3 3.

One High Pair- Any pair Jacks or better.

One Low Pair - Any pair below Jacks.

No Pair - Five odd cards

Some machines contain wild cards, such as a deuce (2) or a Joker. With these machines, Five-of-a-kind hands are paid off, such as a 9 9 9 9 Joker. This hand ranks below a Royal Flush.

Video Poker is basically draw poker, with all cards dealt out by the machine's computer. Five cards are dealt to the player and are shown on the screen.

The player then has the option of holding or discarding as many cards as he wants thus he can hold all five cards or discard all five cards. Or he can hold on to four cards. After he discards some or all of his cards, these are replaced by other cards.

He now has drawn to his hand and this final hand determines whether or not he or she is a winner.

For example, let's suppose that a player has received the following cards at the outset of play:

♠Q ♦7 ♣Q ♠3 ♥6

He has been dealt a pair of queens, which he will hold, while discarding the rest of the cards. That is his best chance of getting the strongest possible hand after the draw. He now discards the 7, 3 and 6 and receives three new cards. Let's assume that his hand now looks like this after the draw:

♠Q ♥Q ♣Q ♠K ♦4

He has improved his hand to Three-of-a-Kind, which means a bigger payout. The stronger the poker hand, the better the payoff.

The machine deals out cards from a 52 card deck, and will never deal a card previously discarded on the same hand. Thus, if a player gets rid of the 6 of clubs, he can't get it back after the draw.

The final hand determines whether or not the player has won or lost. The board will flash **Winner** and show the kind of winning hand it was, such as Three-of-a-Kind, and the payoff. If the hand ended up as a losing hand, nothing will be flashed on the board.

An important consideration, one that should always be kept in mind by the player, is that, although this is draw poker, it is not being played against other players. It is played against the machine, and all one has to do is get hands sufficient for a payoff.

A mistake many experienced draw poker players make is thinking they're beating other players. They'll retain an Ace and get rid of a King, for example, whereas holding both is better to get a payoff in some situations. Or they'll discard a small pair, such as 3s, when those cards should have been held in some situations.

In regular draw poker, it might not pay to hold a low pair, but often, as we shall see later, it's the best play in Video Poker. Always keep in mind that you want to be paid off by the machine, not other players, and therefore, you'll have to alter your strategy to this effect.

Step by Step Play

When you sit down at a Video Poker machine, you'll encounter a number of buttons which allow you to do various things at the machine. But first of all, to make the machine operative, you have to put some coins in.

Video Poker machines take from one to five coins at a time.

We suggest that you always play five coins, never less. On all machines, in order to hit the best payoff on Royal Flushes, it is necessary to have played five coins. If you only have three coins left, go and get more coins, for if you hit the Royal Flush, you'll end up with a much smaller payoff than you should have received. Remember this and remember it well - five coins at all times should be played.

After you put in the five coins, the screen will automatically show five cards dealt in sequence, one next to the other. If you hadn't inserted five coins, but only one to four coins, for example, then in order to have the cards dealt, you'll have to press a button called **Deal/Draw**. Then the five cards will show on the screen. But, if you put in five coins, the cards will automatically be dealt.

Once you see the five cards, you'll also note that the screen will show the various payoffs for various hands to one side of the screen.

The payoffs increase in proportion to the coins played. For example, if Two Pair pays 2 coins for each coin inserted (2 for 1), after five coins are put in, the payoff will read: "Two Pair - 10."

This means that if your final hand is Two Pair, you'll get back or receive credit for 10 coins.

Now let's get back to the five cards shown on the screen. Under each card, on the outside of the machine itself, will be a button that says **Hold/Cancel**. Thus, there will be five of these buttons.

Let's assume that your dealt cards are as follows:

♦3 ♥6 ♣7 ♠10 ♥10

The best possibilities here are the two 10s, which

can be improved in various ways. To hold the two 10s and get rid of the other cards, you press the Hold/Cancel button under each 10.

What if, by accident, you also pressed the Hold/Cancel button under the 3? In that case you press it again, and the Cancel feature will kick in. It will not be held. How can you make sure of what you've held and not held? The word "Held" will show under the cards you've held. Here's how it would look with the previous hand:

♦3 ♥6 ♣7 ♠10 ♥10
HELD HELD

Now that you're satisfied with your held cards, you press another button, called the Deal/Draw button. This will allow you to draw cards to the two 10s. The 3, 6 and 7 will disappear from the screen and will be replaced by the newly drawn cards. Your final hand may look like this:

♣J ♣A ♦J ♠10 ♥10
HELD HELD

You've drawn Two Pair, and the screen will show **"WINNER - Two Pair 10"**, showing that you've ended up with a win of ten coins.

Credits

Most machines will allow you to take credits for the coins won, rather than getting the coins back after each win.

Here's how it works.

After the above win, there'll be a place on the machine for Credits. You'll see **Credit - 10**.

At the same time, a button on the outside of the

machine will light up. It's called a **Cashout** or **Payout** button.

Unless you desire to cash out by pressing this button, the coin credits will stay in the machine, and you can play them out, rather than collect them and put them back into the coin slot. This makes for much faster play, no fumbling for coins, and no dirty hands.

As you continue winning, the credits will increase, and the screen will always show you just how many credits you have.

To continue playing, without inserting additional coins, you now press another button, which may have different names such as **Maximum Bet** or **Bet 5**, but it will be plain that this lit button allows you, by simply pressing it, to use up 5 of your credits.

When you press it, three things will happen.

First, your screen credit total will now read Credit 10 (reduced by 5 from 15). Secondly, the possible winners on your next round of play will flash on one side of the screen, and thirdly, five cards will be dealt to you as the next hand.

You then play the five cards as you did before, trying to get the best possible hand for a payoff from the machine.

What happens if you've been dealt a complete dud, five cards that are low in value and mismatched (called **rags**), so that you don't want to hold any? You simply press the Deal/Draw button and all five cards will disappear from the screen to be replaced by five new ones.

What if the five cards you've been dealt at the outset are such that you don't want to draw any cards to the hand? For example, let's assume that you've been dealt the following hand:

♦4 ♦A ♦3 ♦9 ♦8

You have five diamonds showing, a Flush, an immediate winner, without having to draw additional cards. What you do now is press the Hold/Cancel button under each and every card shown, till there are five HELDS on the screen.

Then you press the Deal/Draw button, and you will see WINNER - Flush as well as the number of coins you've won, flash on the screen.

If you have an immediate winner, such as a Flush, before the draw, *you must hold all the cards to get a payoff.* If you don't press all the Held buttons, and simply press Deal/Draw, the winning cards will disappear from the screen and you'll get five fresh cards.

Now, for the ultimate. What if you end up with a Royal Flush? You'll see **WINNER - ROYAL FLUSH 4000** on the screen. Lights will flash, and the full jackpot of $1,000 (4000 quarters) will be paid to you in cash.

If no one comes by, ring for a change girl or stop one when she goes by. She'll call for a casino executive to verify your win. Then you'll be paid in cash.

If it's a progressive machine the screen will show WINNER - ROYAL FLUSH PROGRESSIVE PAYOUT or a similar statement depending on the machine. If the payoff is above a certain figure ($1,200 on a 25 cents machine) you'll be asked to furnish a social security number and positive identification, and you'll be handed the cash along with a W2-G form to be filed with your next year's income tax.

But let's say that you didn't hit the jackpot but have been winning steadily and now you're tired and want to get away from the machine. The credit reads 125.

You press the CashOut or Payout button and the coins will be released from the machine and drop into the well at the button of the machine. You take them over to a Cashier and they'll be counted and you'll get cash for them.

Go over the steps again carefully.

When you get to a Video Poker machine familiarize yourself with the buttons on the machine.

If there's another button you don't understand the function of, ask a change girl to explain it to you. If she doesn't know, she'll get someone from the casino to help you.

Now that you're familiar with the Video Poker machine, let's move on to the most common of the machines, the one that originally made this game so popular, the Jacks or Better Video Poker Machine.

III. Jacks or Better

Full Payout, Flat-Top & Progressives

Jacks or Better in Video Poker refers to a pair of Jacks, Queens, Kings or Aces. Since the Queen, King or Ace is of a higher rank than the Jack, any pair consisting of these cards is known as Jacks or Better, or a High Pair.

If you get a pair of Jacks, Queens, Kings or Aces as your final hand, five coins will be paid back to you. For example, suppose you end up with a pair of Queens. You'll be declared a WINNER and be given credit for five coins.

Although you're not making any profit since you invested five coins, these returned coins really add up and contributes to making this game almost even-up with the casino when played properly. And we'll show you how to do this.

Once you master Jacks or Better, you'll be able to play the other games of Video Poker more intelligently, and we'll discuss those games in future sections. But the Jacks or Better machines is the one you're most likely to encounter, since they're the most popular of the Video Poker games.

There are two types of Jacks or Better machines, the **Full-Payout** or **Flat-Top** machine, and the **Progressive** machine. The Full-Payout will pay you a fixed amount of coins if you hit the Royal Flush - four thousand coins, provided that you played all five coins.

With the Progressive machine, you'll be paid a jackpot consisting of the amount shown on the Progression, which begins with 4,000 coins or $1,000 on the quarter machines and goes up from there. So, in most cases, if you hit the Royal Flush on the Progressive 25 cents machine, you can expect to cash in from $1,000 to about $3,000, and sometimes more.

There are also slight differences in the payouts between the two machines. Let's first examine the Full-Payout or Flat-Top Machine

Jacks or Better: Full-Payout Machine	
Winning Hand	Payouts Per Coin
Royal Flush	800*
Straight Flush	50
Four of a Kind	25
Full House	9
Flush	6
Straight	4
Three of a Kind	3
Two Pair	2
High Pair	1
*Five coins must be played to get the full payout for the Royal Flush	

Note that five coins must be played, and should always be played, to receive the 800-1 payout for the Royal Flush. All of the payouts mentioned above are to 1 coin. Multiply this by 5 to get the real payout when you play that many coins.

For example, the Royal Flush will pay out 4,000 coins or $1,000, for a quarter machine. Getting a Straight Flush will pay you 250 coins or $62.50 and getting a Full House will pay you 45 coins or $11.25 for that same quarter machine.

These machines are known as 9-6 machines, because of the 9 payout for the Full House and the 6 coin payout for the Flush. By High Pair, we mean Jacks or Better. A pair of 10s will not pay anything back, nor will any lower pair.

Now let's look at the Progressive Payout Machines.

Jacks or Better: Progressive Payouts

Winning Hand	Payouts Per Coin
Royal Flush	Progressive Jackpot*
Straight Flush	50
Four of a Kind	25
Full House	8
Flush	5
Straight	4
Three of a Kind	3
Two Pair	2
High Pair	1

*Five coins must be played to get the full payout for the Royal Flush

This machine is known as an 8-5, because of the payouts for a Full House and a Flush. Again, all payouts shown are for one coin, and so multiply the payout by 5 when five coins have been played.

<u>Always</u> play 5 coins with Progressive machines.

The progressive machines start with a jackpot of $1,000 on quarter machines, exactly the maximum payout on the Full-Payout machines, and goes up from there. The machines are tied to a bank of machines feeding the progressive Jackpot every time a Royal Flush isn't made. Usually about 1% of the money fed into the machines is added to the jackpot each time the game is played. It slowly but surely builds up.

The total of the Jackpot is shown above the bank of machines on a flashing screen. It increases until someone gets the Royal Flush after putting in five coins. If a Royal Flush had been made while someone held less than five coins, the full jackpot is not won and the progression keeps building.

Progressive machines are available, as are Full-Payout machines in 5 cents, 25 cents and $1 denominations. On a 5 cents machine the jackpot starts at $200, and on the $1 machine it begins at $4,000.

To compensate for the progressive aspect of the machine, the payout on the Full House and Flush have been reduced to 8 and 5 instead of the 9 and 6 on the Full-Payout machines.

Winning Strategy for Jacks or Better Machines

These machines can give you an even-up chance

with the house, whether playing the Full-Payout or Progressive machines. But you must play them correctly. Following is the basic strategy against the 8-5 progressive machines. (These strategies are slightly different than 9-6 non-Progressive play.)*

Going For The Royal Flush

Our first goal is to get the Royal Flush, so each time there's a possibility of this occurring, we have to weigh the hands dealt against the chances of drawing to the Royal Flush. Here's our strategy.

1. Whenever we have <u>four cards to a Royal Flush</u>, such as ♣K ♣Q ♣J ♣10 we discard the fifth card, even though it has given us a flush or a straight. For instance, we would discard any other club or any other ace in the above example, except the Ace of clubs.

2. In the above example, if there was another King, Queen, Jack or Ten, giving us a High Pair, we'd discard it, going for the Royal Flush.

3. When we have <u>three to a Royal Flush</u>, we should discard a High Pair and instead draw to the remaining three to a Royal. This is in line with our goal of trying to get that Royal Flush whenever possible.

For example, we're dealt ♦A ♥A ♥K ♥10 ♣3. We'd go for the three cards to a Royal Flush in this situation, breaking up the high pair by throwing away

---

*The full strategy charts for the progressives and 8-5 machines are beyond the scope of this book. Serious players looking for the mathematical edge over the casino and to win money at video poker must buy GRI's Professional Video Poker Strategy advertised in the back pages.

the ♦A (and ♣3), and keeping the ♥A ♥K ♥10.

However, if we hold the following hands, hands that already have a payout on all five cards dealt, we don't go for The Royal Flush.

a. Straight Flush
b. Four of a Kind
c. Full House
d. Three of a Kind

4. When holding a <u>small pair (10s or below) and three to a Royal Flush</u>, we discard the pair and go for the Royal Flush. Example: ♠Q ♠J ♠10 ♦10 ♥4. We discard the ♦10 and ♥4.

5. When we have <u>two to a Royal Flush</u>, we hold all pairs over the possibility of going for the Royal Flush. For example, if we hold ♥A ♦A ♦Q and two **rags** (cards that can't help us) we retain the Aces rather than retaining the two diamonds.

If we hold a low pair and two to the Royal, we still hold onto the low pair, and discard the two cards to the Royal.

6. With <u>two to a Royal</u>, we hold onto four flushes and four straights, Three of a Kinds and Two Pair rather than going for the Royal Flush.

7. If we have <u>two to a Royal</u> and another high card, but no pair, we discard the other high card.

For example, suppose we're dealt ♣Q ♦A ♣K and two rags (small unmatched cards). We discard the ♦A and the rags, going for the Royal with our ♣Q and ♣K.

So, always keep that Royal Flush in mind. It gives us the really big payout, and it's always there lurking in the machine. We can't afford to pass up the opportunity to go for it when the situation favors us.

Straight Flushes, Flushes, Straights

Our best payoff, other than the Royal Flush, is the Straight Flush. However, its payout is merely 50 for 1, or 250 coins against the Royal Flush's payout of 800 coins for 1, or 4, 000 coins.

Therefore, although we're likely to get a Straight Flush four times as often as a Royal Flush, the payout is only 1/16 of the Royal Flush, and even less than 1/16 if a Progressive Jackpot hits.

For example, if the progressive jackpot is $2,000, twice the minimum of 4,000 coins, then the payout on the Straight Flush would be 1/32 of the Royal Flush.

Although we must be aware of the Straight Flush, it's not something we're constantly looking for, as in the case of the Royal.

When we are dealt a Flush, and it contains four to a Straight Flush, such as ♥10 ♥9 ♥8 ♥7 ♥2, our best play is to retain the Flush and not go for the Straight Flush.

If we are dealt a Straight, and it contains four cards to a Straight Flush within it, we stand pat with the Straight. An example would be ♠7 ♠6 ♠5 ♠4 ♦3

A High Pair is always preferable to a four to a Flush or Straight. We retain the High Pair (Jacks or better) and break up the possible Straight or Flush.

With a low pair, we break up the low pair (10s or

lower) in favor of the four to a Flush, but we retain the low pair and break up the four to a Straight.

Four of a Kinds, Full Houses and Three of a Kinds

Four of a Kind hands pay half of what Straight Flushes pay, but occur much more frequently, about once in every 420 hands, or about 22.7 time more frequently than the Straight Flush. Since it pays half of what the Straight Flush pays, it's a much better value for us, coming up so frequently.

Generally, Four of a Kind hands come out of the blue and surprise us. We start our hand with a High Pair or a low pair, and boom! out come two more of the same rank, giving us Four of a Kind.

Or we may stay with Three of a Kind and we get the fourth of that rank. Sometimes, we'll really be surprised by staying with but one high card and getting three more for a Four of a Kind hand!

This is the main difference between regular Draw Poker and Video Poker. In the regular game, we wouldn't stay in with low pairs or just one high card, because it will be a loser in the long run. In Video Poker we have nothing to lose, for we've already invested our money.

Three of a Kind hands occur about once every thirteen times we're dealt hands, or about 7.5% of the time. We may get them by retaining a low or High Pair, or start with Three of a Kind.

Or perhaps, if we're fortunate, we've stayed in with one High Card and received two more of the same rank after the draw.

We always stay for the draw with a Three of a Kind hand. It's much stronger for us than three to a Royal Flush, so if we're dealt ♥K ♥Q ♥10 ♣10 ♦10, we retain the three 10s and discard the King and Queen of hearts.

A Full House is often made from a hand that starts as a Three of a Kind hand. Or it may develop from a Two Pair hand, where the odds are roughly 11-1 against this happening.

Of course, like all hands in Video Poker, a Full House may come out of the blue, where we've retained one low pair, such as ♦5 ♠5 and see the draw produce ♣J ♦J ♠J

A Full House occurs a little over 1% of the time.

Two Pair, High Pairs and Low Pairs

Two Pairs occur about once every 7.6 hands and pays off with only two coins for one invested or in reality, even-money. Thus, we get back 10 coins for the five coins we played, the five we invested plus the five won.

We always retain an original hand of Two Pair hoping for a Full House at best, though the odds are about 11-1 against this occurring.

A High Pair allows us to get our original investment back each time the hand comes up.

Although this doesn't seem like much, it is the reason for the game's popularity, for it enables players to constantly get payouts and thus retain their bankroll till the big payouts come through.

Never underestimate the power of the High Pair.

We should be dealt one about every 4.6 hands.

We retain the High Pair when it is part of a possible Straight or Flush, and discard the other cards in those situations.

However, if there's four to the Royal Flush or three to the Royal Flush, the High Pair would be discarded in favor of possibly getting the Royal Flush.

If the High Pair is part of a Straight Flush, such as ♦J ♦10 ♦9 ♦8 ♣J then we get rid of the ♣J in this situation and go for the Straight Flush. We also do this even if the possible Straight Flush can be made by drawing to it as an inside Straight Flush, as in the following situation:

♥Q ♥J ♥10 ♥8 ♠Q

In the above example, the ♠Q would be thrown away. There's a chance for a Straight Flush, a Flush, a Straight, and another High Pair when this is done, giving us more powerful hands to go for, with bigger payouts.

With small pairs, we have hands that give us a great many payouts when they are improved. Normally, in regular draw poker, only a very weak player would retain a pair of deuces, but in Video Poker, those deuces can turn into Three-of-a-Kind hands or better if we get a lucky draw.

When do we retain small pairs? First of all, if the rest of the hand is blank, (filled with rags, trash cards of no value to us). For example:

♠3 ♦10 ♥8 ♥5 ♣3

The best we have here is the pair of black 3s. We'd hold the 3s and draw to them.

If the low pair comes as part of a Flush, we discard the odd paired card and draw to our four Flush, as in the following example:

♣7 ♣9 ♣3 ♣A ♦9

We get rid of the ♦9 and draw to the remaining clubs hoping for a Flush.

However, if we have a Low Pair and it's part of a possible Straight, we hold onto the Low Pair and draw to it, such as ♦6 ♠6 ♦7 ♠8 ♣9

In this case, we discard the ♦7 ♣8 ♣9.

We also discard the Low Pair if the remaining cards are three to a Royal Flush.

If we have a Low Pair, and it's part of a three to a Straight Flush, as in the following example, we retain the Low Pair.

♣8 ♣7 ♣6 ♦6 ♥2

The correct play is to hold the pair of 6s.

Other Hands

Most of the time, the hands dealt to you at the outset of play, before the draw, won't be winners by themselves. You'll have to improve them to get a payout. Some of the hands will be so bad that you'll discard all five cards and draw five new ones.

At times you'll find yourself with a beautiful drawing hand that comes up empty. For example:

♠A ♠Q ♠J ♠K ♦3

Having four to a Royal Flush, we discard the ♦3 and draw, hoping for the BIG ONE! Instead, we draw a 9 of hearts and end up without a payout of any kind.

Other good hands will end up as blanks for us. This is to be expected. Don't get discouraged. There will be other times, as there was for this author, when the following hand was dealt to him at the outset:

♦4 ♥7 ♦9 ♠2 ♣J

Faced with this pile of garbage, I retained the ♣J, the only viable play. Imagine my surprise when I drew and the screen showed the following:

♣K ♣Q ♣10 ♣ A ♣J

HELD

And on the screen was the flash:

WINNER! JACKPOT! ROYAL FLUSH!

That can happen, so the big ones that get away shouldn't stop you from continuing to play. Sooner or later, your lucky moment may come.

When dealt hands that aren't immediate winners before the draw, we first have to look for the possibility of a Royal Flush. For example, if we're dealt the following:

♣3 ♦10 ♠6 ♥9 ♦K

We save both the ♦10 ♦K. We have two to a Royal, and that's our best shot, even though, if the 10 gets paired, we won't get our money back. We're always looking for the Royal.

Many times we'll get a hand like this:

♦4 ♥A ♣J ♠6 ♥3

We hold the ♥A ♣J here, for we're trying to pair one of these to get our coins back. Many Players make the mistake of retaining only the Ace and discarding the Jack. That's a bad play. Hold onto both.

The reason they make this common error is that they think they're back playing Draw Poker against friends - where retaining the Ace because it's stronger than the Jack might be playable.

But in Video Poker, the Ace has no more value

25

than the Jack; either paired will get our coins back.

Here are a listing of other hands that should be drawn to when dealt at the outset. None of these are immediate winners.

- <u>Four to a Flush</u>
- <u>Four to a Straight</u>
- <u>Four to Straight Flush</u>, whether the missing card is on the inside of the possible Straight Flush or not. For example, ♥9 ♥8 ♥7 ♥5 and a rag. Go for the Straight Flush here. Of course since you have a Four to a Flush, you'll automatically draw to this hand in the proper way.
- <u>Three to a Straight Flush</u>. If you're dealt cards that contain at least three to the Straight Flush, discard the rags and go for it. If the hand contains a high card as part of the Straight Flush, it is that much stronger, such as ♣J ♣10 ♣9, since the Jack may be paired.
- <u>A low pair</u>. We've touched on this hand before. It's a very common starting hand, and can develop into a monster after the draw. Just because it doesn't pay automatically doesn't mean you get rid of it. When dealt the following:

♣ 5 ♦5 ♥A ♣J ♦ 10

We retain the pair of 5s, which are stronger for us than the Ace of hearts and Jack of clubs.

Now let's deal with those hands that are so bad there's no reason to hold any of the cards. When we get five blanks or rags, we discard all the cards and go for five new cards on the draw. A typical hand might be this:

♥2 ♦6 ♣10 ♦5 ♥9

There's nothing worth holding. We don't save two

to a Straight or two to a Flush, or even, in this situation, two to a Straight Flush. They're just not strong enough hands.

We don't save the highest valued card of the five, the club 10, because even if it's paired, it won't give us any return. We discard all the cards, and draw five new ones. To do this, simply press the Deal/Draw button and five new cards will appear on the screen. If the 10 of clubs had been the Jack of clubs, we'd have retained the Jack. If paired, it would return our money.

Don't be afraid to get rid of all five cards if they're weak and start with five new cards after the draw. There's always the possibility of getting a payoff of some kind, or even a tremendous payout after a draw like that.

I saw someone get Four of a Kind drawing to five new cards. It's even possible to get a Royal Flush when doing this!

Some Winning Hints

We have discussed the fact that Video Poker is a different game than regular Draw Poker.

One of the important differences is this - when you play Draw Poker at home or in a casino and you're dealt five cards, the first thing most players do is sort their cards. If they've been dealt a pair, they put them together. If they have four to a Straight, those cards are placed together in sequence.

However, when playing Video Poker, the cards come up on the screen just as the computer deals them, and the player can't sort them out by hand, only in his or her mind. So, you've got to be super-careful about not overlooking a strong hand.

Here's an example of a hand I saw a player overlook before the draw:

$$\diamond 5 \ \heartsuit 6 \ \clubsuit 3 \ \diamond 2 \ \spadesuit 4$$

Dealt these five low cards, he pressed the Deal/Draw button immediately to draw five new cards, overlooking a straight.

Or the hand might look like this:

$$\clubsuit 4 \ \diamond 3 \ \spadesuit A \ \heartsuit 5 \ \clubsuit 2$$

In this situation a player told me he saw someone hold the Ace and get rid of all his other cards, overlooking a Straight.

Therefore, my best advice is to slow down a bit and examine the cards that have been dealt at the outset and see just what you have on the screen. Take your time in determining the correct play.

Remember, if you make a mistake, and hold a card you don't want to hold, you can rectify that mistake by pressing the Hold/Cancel button, and the card will no longer be held. As long as you don't press the Deal/Draw button, you still have a chance to change your mind.

Even experienced veterans of the game make mistakes. They may be weary or tired or upset and they can, in this state, overlook obvious plays. If you reach a point where the game has become tedious, leave the machine and cash in. Take a break and a rest and go back another time

Practicing At Home

To familiarize yourself with correct play in Jacks or Better, my advice is not to go to a casino unless you've practiced the game at home. To do this is simplicity itself.

Get a standard deck of cards and remove the Jokers. This leaves you with 52 cards. Shuffle them thoroughly and then deal out five card hands to yourself, one at a time.

After you've dealt out five cards, look over the hand and decide what to hold and what to discard. For example, you might deal this hand:

♣A ♦3 ♦6 ♥K ♣9

In this situation, you'd hold the ♣A and ♥K and discard the other three cards.

Discard the cards by putting them aside, not back in the deck. When you play Video Poker, the machine will not deal you a card you've already discarded, and neither should you do this at home.

Then draw three cards. You may take them right off the top of the deck or shuffle up the remaining cards and pick out three at random. It really doesn't matter how you do this.

After you've dealt out the three additional cards as your draw, see what has developed, whether or not you'd have gotten a payout. You can keep a record of your wins and losses, meanwhile refining and correcting your play.

After you're comfortable with the game and feel you know what you're doing, then you can go to a casino and play for real money.

IV. Testing Your Knowledge of Jacks or Better

The following is a small quiz to refine and test your knowledge of the game played in the casino. We'll assume we're at a Progressive Jacks or Better machine with an 8-5 payout on the Full House and Flush, respectively.

Decide how to play each of the following hands:

1. ♣5 ♦5 ♠A ♥9 ♦10

We hold the pair of 5s and discard all other cards. Players are tempted to hold the Ace as a "kicker" hoping to pair it, but don't hold kickers in Video Poker. It's a losing proposition.

2. ♦9 ♦K ♣K ♦8 ♦2

We hold the two Kings and get rid of all the other diamonds. Our best play when facing a four to a Flush with a High Pair, is to retain the High Pair.

3. ♣K ♣A ♣Q ♣10 ♠J

With four to the Royal Flush, we discard the spade Jack. Whenever we have four to a Royal we're going for that big payout. Break up the Straight in this situation.

4. ♠Q ♦3 ♠J ♥K ♥2

This is a common situation. We have three High cards, but two of those are of the same suit. In this situation, we get rid of the High card not of the same suit. Thus, we'd hold the Queen and Jack of spades and dump the heart King.

We're giving ourselves a shot at the Royal Flush and giving up the chance of pairing the King in this situation. Of course, we're giving up a three to a Straight, but going after the Royal is a better bet.

5. ♠9 ♥5 ♥2 ♥8 ♣3

We hold nothing out of this pile of garbage. Even though we have three to a Flush, there's no reason to overcome the great odds in getting the flush by drawing two to it. We're better off going for five fresh cards after the draw.

6. ♠10 ♣8 ♦3 ♠J ♠4

At first glance, it would seem that we hold the spade Jack and discard the other cards. Or we should take a long shot and hold all three spades.

Both of these decision are incorrect. What we have to do here is hold both the spade Jack and the spade 10. Although the 10, if paired, gives us nothing, the 10 and Jack gives us two to the Royal. A much stronger play than merely holding the spade Jack.

7. ♠2 ♥A ♣K ♦J ♣2

We hold the deuces and discard the three big cards. A small pair is powerful in Video Poker. There's a possibility of getting Two Pair, Three of a Kind, a Full House and even Four of a Kind. When we have a small pair, we don't chase after the possibility of pairing a big card. And we don't hold kickers.

8. ♥Q ♦J ♠10 ♠4 ♠3

With this hand, we have three to a Flush and three to a Straight. However, we also have a Queen and Jack, which, if paired, will get our coins back. We therefore hold the Queen and Jack and discard the other cards.

9. ♣K ♦9 ♣J ♣Q ♠9

Here we have three to a Royal Flush plus a small pair of 9s. Whenever we have this situation, a low pair opposed to a three to a Royal, we get rid of the low pair and hold the three to a Royal Flush.

10. ♥K ♥Q ♥10 ♥J ♥5

Here we have four to a Royal Flush, as well as a formed Flush. In this situation, we get rid of the heart 5 and go for the Royal Flush.

Why? Just look at the odds. Suppose the Progressive payout at this point is $1,600 for $1.25 or 1,280 for 1.

Even though we already have the Flush in hand, the chances of getting the Ace of hearts and completing our Royal is only 46-1. We know five of the 52 cards, and thus, with 47 cards remaining, one of them is the Ace of spades.

We're taking a chance at winning 1,280 for 1 by going for a 46-1 shot.

We could go on and on with the quiz. However, you can test yourself by playing out hands at home as advised in the Practice At Home section.

If you practice enough, there are sure to be all kinds of hands that you'll have to pause and think about. Study our book and you'll know what to do, so that, by the time you get to the casino, you'll be ready to play correctly.

And if you want to learn Video Poker so that you can play on a professional level and actually have an edge over the casino, there's an excellent advanced strategy in the back of the book.

V. Tens or Better

This type of machine is rarely found in casinos. Sometimes only $1 machines can be found. There are occasional Progressive machines available with very low payoffs on the regular hands other than the Royal Flush and they're generally avoided by experts.

The following is the payout on the non-progressive machines. Note that the Royal Flush is paid at 800-1 only if five coins have been played.

10s or Better: Full-Payout Machine	
Winning Hand	Payouts Per Coin
Royal Flush	800*
Straight Flush	50
Four of a Kind	25
Full House	6
Flush	5
Straight	4
Three of a Kind	3
Two Pair	2
High Pair (10s - Aces)	1
*Five coins must be played to get the full payout for the Royal Flush	

This machine pays off only 6 units for a Full House, compared to 9 units on the Jacks or Better machines, and only 5 units instead of 6 for the Flush. However, this is made up by returning the coins played whenever the players gets a pair of 10s.

Play is pretty much the same as for Jacks or Better; however, 10s are retained instead of discarded as they are in Jacks or Better.

VI. Deuces Wild

The Wild Card

Like the other versions of Video Poker, the game is played with the 52-card deck used without the jokers. However, each of the four deuces (2s) is a **wild card**, which means that it can be used as any card in the deck, not only in rank (such as a 5 or 6, for example) but as any suit.

Thus, a 2 of clubs can be transferred, if needed, to an Ace of spades to complete a Royal Flush. Since there are four deuces in the deck, hands containing at least one deuce have been calculated to occur about 35% of the time.

The following is the payout for Deuces Wild Video Poker. Note that the Royal Flush as a natural hand (without the deuces) will be paid off at 800-1 only if five coins are played.

Deuces Wild Video Poker Payout

Winning Hand	Payouts Per Coin
Royal Flush (Natural)	800*
Four Deuces	200
Royal Flush (Deuces)	25
Five of a Kind	15
Straight Flush	9
Four of a Kind	5
Full House	3
Flush	2
Straight	2
Three of a Kind	1

*Five coins must be played to get the full payout for the Royal Flush

After the normal arrangement of hands in Jacks or Better Video Poker, the Deuces Wild version of Video Poker must seem upside down. For example, the weakest possible hand with a payout is Three of a Kind. And a Five of a Kind hand pays only 15 for 1! With the deuces running wild in the deck, all kinds of crazy hand can be made.

Playing Deuces Wild can be a roller coaster ride with wild streaks coming and going, both favorable and unfavorable. When the deuces show up on the screen, all kinds of payouts are possible. When they're absent, it's a desert out there, because of the low payouts on relatively strong hands, such as 2 for 1 (even-money) for a Flush.

With Deuces Wild, you must be patient and not get discouraged with a long losing streak. Even if dealt one deuce, your chances of making a hand that pays out is only 54%.

With three deuces, you can expect to have some very strong hands, with about 80% of them being Four of a Kind or stronger.

Deuces Wild Video Poker Strategy

First and foremost, when we have a deuce or deuces dealt to us, we must evaluate our hands carefully for the strongest possible hands. Very powerful hands in deuces wild aren't obvious with deuces showing, so pay careful attention to the following hands.

1. If we have three deuces and two to a Royal Flush, that's a Royal Flush and should be held intact.

2. With two deuces and three to a Royal Flush, that's a Royal Flush and should be held intact.

3. Two deuces and Three of a Kind is a Five of a Kind hand and should be held intact.

4. If we have two deuces and three cards to a Flush, it is a Flush (and possibly a Straight Flush) and should be held intact.

5. Two deuces and any pair gives us Four of a Kind and should be held intact.
  • With two deuces and three odd cards, none of which can give you a Royal Flush, draw 3 cards to the deuces.
  • With two deuces, if you have 2 other cards to a

Royal or Straight Flush, and one blank, discard the blank and go for the Royal or Straight Flush.
• With 2 deuces and any single card (10, J, Q, K or A) that will give you a Royal Flush, retain this card.

6. With a single deuce and three to a Royal Flush plus a blank, we discard the odd card (blank) and draw. Example: 2 ♣A ♣K ♣J ♦4 - we discard the 4 of diamonds and draw one card.

7. Without a deuce, if the hand is pat, that is, already assures us a payout with all five cards involved, we hold all five cards and do not draw.

8. Without a deuce, we hold four card Straights and four card Flushes and four card Straight Flushes and draw.

9. Without a deuce, we hold three card Straight Flushes, and draw.

10. If we have been dealt Two Pair at the outset, we discard one of the pairs. We do this because Two Pair doesn't pay anything. With One Pair retained, we can improve that to Three of a Kind or higher valued hands with our without the addition of a deuce.
Many of the hands in Jacks or Better become money payout hands just by pairing a high card (a Jack or better). In Deuces Wild, these hands have no value to us. Getting One Pair or even Two Pair gives us nothing but a loser. We must constantly strive for

the big hands. If we have a deuce or more than one deuce we must study the situation carefully to get our biggest possible hands, then play for those big hands.

Now, what do we do with weaker hands? For example, suppose we're dealt the following hand:

$$\heartsuit A \;\; \diamondsuit K \;\; \clubsuit Q \;\; \diamondsuit 4 \;\; \heartsuit 9$$

We'd get rid of all five cards in this situation. Our goal is to get at least a Three of a Kind hand and none of these cards will help us. High cards have no preference over low cards here - there's no special coin return for High Pairs.

Suppose we have the following hand:

$$\heartsuit Q \;\; \diamondsuit K \;\; \clubsuit 9 \;\; \spadesuit 5 \;\; 2$$

Again, we discard all the cards except the deuce. Having a high pair does us no good. Three cards to a Straight or Flush does us no good. We hold the deuce and hope for the best.

You're going to find yourself getting rid of all five cards in Deuces Wild quite often, as much as 25% of the time. This is to be expected, since we need that big Three of a Kind hand just to get our coins back.

Play the game correctly and you'll be rewarded with all kinds of big hands, and if you encounter a good winning streak, this game can earn you some good money even without hitting the Royal Flush.

VII. Jokers Wild

Ace-King and Two Pairs

In casinos you're going to come across this game played in two versions. The first is known as **Ace-King** and the second as **Two Pairs**. In the first version of the game, any pair of Aces or King will get our money back, while in the second version of the game, the minimum winning hand is Two Pairs.

With the addition of the Joker, we now have a deck containing 53 cards, with approximately 10% more different kinds of hands dealt out than in the standard 52 card Video Poker games.

Since there's only one joker, the hands aren't as complicated to figure out as Deuces Wild Video Poker, where all four deuces run rampant. Still, it's a more complex game, with a more complicated payout scale.

Let's examine the payouts, and as usual, keep in mind that the Royal Flush can only be paid off with the maximum return if five coins are played.

Joker Wild Payout (Ace-King)

Winning Hand	Payouts Per Coin
Royal Flush (Natural)	800*
Five of a Kind	200
Royal Flush (Joker)	100
Straight Flush	50
Four of a Kind	20
Full House	7
Flush	5
Straight	3
Three of a Kind	2
Two Pair	1
Aces or Kings	1

*Five coins must be played to get the full payout for the Royal Flush

Note that there's the same payout whether one gets a pair of Aces or Kings, or Two Pair. The most popular of the Joker Wild game in this version is played as a 25¢ machine.

A version of the above game which should be avoided by players, features only a payout of 15 for 1 for Four of a Kind. Don't play this machine, but look for one with a full payout of 20 for 1.

The lack of payout for any hand below Two Pair in Joker Wild - Two Pair makes this a machine many experts avoid. When the Joker doesn't appear at the outset, before the draw, there are going to be many hands that will not get any payout whatsoever.

The machine, however, is available to be played for 5 cents, which makes it popular despite the tough payout schedule.

Joker Wild Payout (Two Pair)

Winning Hand	Payouts Per Coin
Royal Flush (Natural)	1000*
Five of a Kind	100
Royal Flush (Joker)	50
Straight Flush	50
Four of a Kind	20
Full House	8
Flush	7
Straight	5
Three of a Kind	2
Two Pair	1

*Five coins must be played to get the full payout for the Royal Flush

And some machines have a **Double Up** feature, which allows the player to take the original payout or try for a double or nothing situation. Since a double or nothing option gives the house no advantage, being a 50-50 proposition, the return is increased to the point where it is almost an even game with the casino.

Joker Wild - Aces and Kings Strategy

The Joker will appear in the hand less than 10% of the time, or about 9.4%. Without the Joker present there will be many instances where the five cards dealt at the outset will have to be discarded. Since only Aces and Kings are good as High Pairs, we don't retain Queens or Jacks. They're as useless as very small pairs.

When playing without the Joker present at the

outset, we will break up a Straight to go for the Straight Flush. Thus, a hand consisting of ♥9 ♥8 ♥7 ♥6 ♣5 will be broken up. The ♣5 will be discarded and one card will be drawn to the hand.

If we have a three to a Royal Flush, we prefer that hand to a pair of Aces or Kings. For example, ♦J ♦ A ♦Q ♣ A ♠5 will be broken up as follows: The ♠5 and the ♣ A will be discarded and we'll go with our three to a Royal Flush.

Without the Joker, not only will many hands be discarded, but the following hands should also be completely discarded, with nothing held for the draw:

- Two cards to a Flush
- Three cards to a Flush, unless it gives us a chance at a Royal Flush, such as A J 10, or a Straight Flush, such as 9 7 6.

The strategical considerations for this game are complicated by the fact that there are often two different ways to play the hand; one with the Joker and one without.

There is a strong likelihood of getting Straight Flushes with the Joker. Therefore, a Joker which forms a Flush will be broken up if there's a possibility of a Straight Flush. Such a hand would be:

Jkr ♥7 ♥6 ♥ 5 ♥Q

We get rid of the Queen and forfeit the 5 for 1 payout in the hope of getting the 50 for 1 payoff for the Straight Flush.

A similar situation occurs when we have:

Jkr ♦5 ♦6 ♦J ♣9.

Here we discard both the ♦J and the ♣9 going for the possible Straight Flush with the Joker and the two other remaining low diamonds.

Likewise, a Straight containing the Joker will be broken up in favor of a four card Straight Flush.

With a Joker present at the outset of play, we have many chances at a Straight Flush and should keep this in mind. For example, if we have a Joker with a high card (Ace or King) we break it up if there's a possibility of getting a Straight Flush even if we only have three to the Straight Flush.

An example of this would be:

Jkr ♦A ♣9 ♣8 ♠7

In the above instance, we discard the diamond Ace and Spade 7 and draw for the Straight Flush. We would keep a Straight made with the Joker unless there is a possibility of getting a Straight Flush by having four to the Straight Flush. An example of this hand is the following:

♠7 Jkr ♠6 ♠5 ♦4

We discard the ♦4 and try for our Straight Flush. Again, we give up the chance for a 5 for 1 payout in favor of the possible 50 for 1 payoff.

Many times, when dealt the Joker with other cards, we'll discard all the other cards and play for the draw with just the Joker remaining. This will happen about 10% of the time and will include the following hands:

• The hand, including the Joker, only contains three cards to a Flush. Keep the Joker only.

• The hand, including the Joker, only contains two cards to a Straight Flush. Keep the Joker only.

• There's no chance for a Royal Flush.

Most of the time we'll be playing hands that go for the Straight Flush or Royal Flush. Or we'll be

43

going for Flushes and Straights, holding three cards with the Joker. We'd hold Three of a Kind hands, Straights and Full Houses, together with stronger hands, of course.

Jokers Wild is a good game to play, because it's essentially an even game with the casino. But you must master it by studying this section carefully, to get your best shot against the house.

Winning Strategy
for Joker Wild - Two Pair

This is a very tough game to beat when the Joker doesn't show up. The need for Two Pair for a payout gives the casino its biggest edge over the player in any of the Video Poker games, unless the Double Up feature is present. That feature allows us to go for double or nothing after play, and brings the machine up to the standard of other Video Poker games, with less than a 1% edge to the house.

Like its partner, the Jokers Wild game, there is a strong likehood of getting Straight Flushes and the strategy for going for them is identical to that game.

One big difference. A Straight won't be broken up to go for a potential Straight Flush, unless there's also the possibility of getting a Royal Flush. With the Joker giving us three cards to the Royal Flush, we hold that in favor of a four to a Flush, four to a Straight and a single Pair.

When a Joker is dealt in this game, we should avoid playing it alone, as we do in the Ace and King version of Joker Wild. It is to our advantage to hold onto the Joker and a 10, Jack, Queen, King or Ace and go for the Royal Flush.

Three to a Straight Flush or Royal Flush are important hands for us to play for the draw, especially if we haven't yet been dealt the Joker. The Joker gives us a wide opportunity to fill in the Straight and Royal Flushes.

VIII. Money Management

Video Poker Machines

You'll be encountering Video Poker machines that take nickels, quarters and dollars. By far, the most common and popular machines are the 25¢ ones. They offer a good payout, and the risk of losing big money is much less than the $1 machines.

The Bankroll

When playing any kind of machine, whether 5¢, 25¢ or $1 ones, we suggest that you have sufficient funds to carry you through a long session of play. To do this, we advise our players to have at least 200 coins of whatever denomination they're playing. With nickels, that amounts to $10; quarters will require a

$50 investment, and dollars a $200 bankroll. This will give you sufficient play for quite a while, unless you hit an immediate crushing losing streak, which is very rare.

However, you have the chance of hitting a winning streak as well, where you'll start with credits after playing the first five coins and never have to dig in again. You can't know what the future brings in terms of gambling; you have to see what happens, and play the very best you can.

There's another good reason why you should have this many coins. You may be onto a good machine that you feel is going to feed you the Royal Flush. Perhaps you've come close a few times, with four to the Royal showing up.

You just feel in your bones that it will happen soon - that big payout! But you find that you started with only twenty or forty coins and now you have to find a change girl or go to the cashier's cage across the casino to get more coins.

If you have to get up, and there's someone sitting next to you, you may have to ask them to hold your seat. If they agree, to further strengthen your claim to the seat, you may invert a container that holds coins, and put it on the seat. Then you get up and go for the additional coins.

However, when you come back, someone else is sitting in that seat, and the neighbor, a stranger you didn't know, shrugs his or her shoulders, or is no longer playing. And while you're standing there getting ready to argue, the guy in your seat hits the Royal Flush!!!

That's a nightmare come true. So, give yourself leeway with enough coins to carry you through a long session. Start with even more coins, 400 coins. All it is is some additional weight, which you can put away in the well of the machine or in a nearby container.

If you don't use up the coins, just cash them in at the end of play. The casino doesn't care. They'll take them back without question.

Of course, before you play any machines, make sure that you can afford to lose the money you're gambling with. Although these machines will give you a chance to break even with the house, short term fluctuations may swing wildly one way or another.

When to Quit

A principle of gambling that is wisdom to all concerned is "the first loss is the cheapest."

If you start with your bankroll of 100 coins and lose it, quit. Something is wrong with your luck that day, and you don't want to take a big single beating that you will find hard to make up.

If you're winning, then you have to decide just when to quit. There are several factors that may play a role. First of all, you may be at a machine that is seducing you with fours to a Royal Flush coming up time and time again. If you have a feeling that it may come up, keep playing even though you're winning big. By big, we mean upwards of 150 credits.

With the credit feature of the machine, you can easily see just how you're doing.

If you feel fresh, keep playing the machine. But if you find yourself making mistakes through fatigue, stop playing, no matter how much you're winning or losing. It's time to take a break or pack it in for the day. Don't fight fatigue.

To insure a winning session, when you hit the 150 credits mark, you may want to put away 50 of those coins, and play the remainder of the 100 left. Since the payout button doesn't work that way, but pays out all the credits, you simply make a mind decision to stop when the credits hit 100, then cash out.

If you hit the 200 mark after making this decision, you can up the win to 125. If the machine turns cold and gets down to 125, you cash out. If the machine, however, continues hot, with all kinds of big hands coming up one after the other, stick with the machine.

Maybe it will get up to 350. By then, you've decided to cash out when the machine fall to 275. By making these mind stops on the way up, you'll have the advantage of playing on with the "hot" machine, and being assured of leaving the machine a winner.

But again, do this only if you don't get fatigued and make mistakes.

If you never reach that 150 mark, but hover around the 60-100 mark in winnings, you may decide that, if the machine drops to 50, you're going to cash out the credits. Again, you'll assure yourself of a nice win.

If the machine never gets above 50 in credits you may decide to leave when the machine credits drop to 0, so as to limit your losses to the few coins you've played.

The figures we've mentioned are just "ball park"

figures. You may want to set a goal of 120 credits, for example, and then quit if it goes down to 60 or 70. Fine. You might want to cash it all in if you ever reach 200 credits. Not so fine. I'd always give myself some leeway.

I'd set the mind goal at 30-40 credits below that figure if you're conservative and leave then (if the credits now are 160-170).

This is known as "stop-loss" playing, and those of you who own stocks know about this concept. You won't hit the top in winnings, but you'll give yourself the chance to keep adding to the winnings.

I've seen players move up like that, till they were in the 400 credit range, when their initial goal had been 150 credits. The machine was hot and kept hitting big hands. You don't get those kind of machines every day of the week, so take advantage of them.

What if you hit the Royal Flush?

You'll be paid in cash by an executive of the casino for the Royal. After you're paid, look to see if there are still credits remaining in the machine. They're yours and shouldn't be left there in the excitement of the moment.

Cash in those credits (but only after you're paid for the Royal) and don't play that machine anymore. It's done it's job, giving you the Royal. Take a break and try another machine if you're still feeling lucky.

Play a machine in another area of the casino, and see if you can repeat your big win!

IX. Selecting the Best Machine

Selecting Machines

Any type of machine you select, among those we've discussed, will give you about an even-money shot against the casino. Of course, you want more than that; you want to get a big win. Your best chance at this is to get the Royal Flush, and get it on a Progressive machine.

When you go into a casino, it'll look like a forest of metal, with slot machines predominating. If you don't see any Video Poker machines, ask a Change person to help you out. They'll know where they're located.

Then study the kinds of machines they have there. If they're some new exotic machine you don't understand, don't play them. But generally speaking, you're bound to find the Jacks or Better machines, which we feel is the easiest to play and gives as good a return as any other.

You may find one to two types of Jack or Better. There will either be the Full Payout type or the Progressive machine. Now, make certain that the coins denomination necessary to play the machine is within your bankroll.

If you're inexperienced, don't attempt the $1 machines. It might be better for you to practice on the 5¢ ones. Usually, the machine you'll encounter the most will be the 25¢ one.

Jacks or Better Machines

If the machine is a Full Payout one, make certain that it is of the 9-6 variety; that is, it pays off at 9 for 1 on the Full House and 6 for 1 on the Flush. If it is a Full Payout machine and only pays off at 8-5 on those hands, don't play it. The house is taking too much of an edge.

If you find a Progressive machine, it will pay out at 8-5 for the Full House and Flush, and the jackpot for getting the Royal Flush will begin at $1,000.

The jackpot progressive amount will be displayed on a screen above a bank of machines tied up to that Progression. Since it begins at $1,000, if it shows an amount like $1,014.66 you can be sure the Royal Flush has been recently hit.

Try and play a progressive machine that's much higher than that in terms of the Royal Flush payout. A machine that shows $1,400 is better, of course, and even better is one that's $1,800 or over $2,000.

If there are only $1 machines available, and you either have a limited bankroll or don't want to risk that kind of bet, don't play the machines.

If there are only 5¢ machines, and you want at least a quarter machine, don't play the 5¢ ones. You may have an attitude - "I just want to kill some time and lose a few bucks." That shouldn't be your stance - you should always think of making money at Video Poker.

Let's assume that you found a bank of Video Poker machines that is agreeable to you. They're Progressive Jacks or Better, played for 25¢ and the present Jackpot is over $2,000.

Bringing Enough Change

Get change for your cash, with sufficient coins to give yourself a long session with the chance of hitting the Royal Flush.

These progressives are extremely popular and you may find only a couple of seats open. Which of the two seats should you take? That's difficult to answer. You're there; you have to make the decision.

I watched a friend play at a Progressive machine in one of the downtown Las Vegas casinos. There were only two seats available and the jackpot was $1,666. The two empty seats were next to each other.

He hesitated and then selected one of them. He started to feed the machine coins and quickly used up a $10 roll of quarters. Nothing came up for him. Nothing.

Meanwhile, a middle-aged man took the other empty seat. He hit a Full House the first shot, then a Flush, then Three of a Kind, and two more Full Houses.

My friend meanwhile had used up $30 worth of quarters. He opened another roll, while looking around for a different seat.

"I hate this machine," he told me. "Look at this guy next to me. Why didn't I pick that machine. "

The man next to him had over 240 credits showing and continued to hit good hands.

My friend, with a disgusted gesture, put in his five coins, and out came the following hand:

♦Q   ♣K   ♣J   ♥3   ♠4

He correctly discarded the heart 3, spade 4 and the diamond Queen, foregoing the possibility of pairing the Queen, against the possibility of drawing three to a Royal. Out came the following:

♣A   ♣K   ♣J   ♣10   ♣Q

      HELD HELD

Bells started ringing, and my friend was $1,666 richer. So you never know.

Some players jump around from machine to machine as their luck turns sour; others stick with the same machine. People are superstitious and many are afraid to switch machines, fearing that the person taking their place will immediately hit the Royal.

But you have to use your own instincts. And perhaps you'll be correct and be grinning from ear to ear as the big payout comes along!

X. A Final Note

Follow the principles we've outlined carefully. First, practice at home before attempting to play in a casino. Play at a monetary level that you find comfortable and don't play $1 machines on a 25¢ bankroll.

Take enough coins to the machine in advance, so that you can play for a sufficient time. Play to win.

Always put in five coins. If you're down to only three coins, for example, hold the seat and get two additional coins to play, or don't play the three at all. The one thing you don't want to do is hit a Royal Flush with less than the necessary five coins to effect the big payout.

When playing for a long time, you may get thirsty. Casinos will generally treat their Video Poker customers well. By ringing for a waitress, you'll be entitled to free drinks. Take advantage of this service if you have a long session at the machines, and don't forget to tip the waitress.

Leave when fatigued. Leave a winner, if possible. Play correctly and you're not only going to have a lot of fun with Video Poker, you're going to be a winner!

XI. Glossary of Video Poker

Cancel Button - A button that allows a player to cancel a previous decision he has made, such as holding a card before the draw. If "HELD" has flashed on the screen, pressing the cancel button will erase it.

Cash Out Button - A button that releases the credits and drops all previously won coins into the well.

Changeperson - A casino employee who makes change so the player can use a machine. Also the employee who pays off the player in bills after coins are presented to him or her.

Credit Button - This button enables the player to play out credits accumulated rather than constantly place additional coins into the machine. Most machines allow the player either to use one credit at a time or the maximum allowed on the machine, such as five credits.

Deal Button - After coins are put into the machine, pressing this button shows the new hand dealt. It may be pressed at any time after one or more coins are placed into the machine, but using maximum credits instead of putting coins into the machine will negate the use of the Deal Button, for the hand will automatically be displayed.

Deuces Wild - A form of Video Poker in which each deuce (2) is a wild card.

Draw Button - By pressing this button, the player draws new cards to his hand, replacing those he has not held. A player may replace all the cards in the original hand if he so wishes.

Flattop Machines - These machines have a fixed maximum payout, which is usually 4,000 coins for a Royal Flush.

Four Flush - A hand consisting of four cards of the same suit, such as 10♠ 5♠ 9♠ K♠, together with an odd card.

Four of a Kind - A hand consisting of four cards of the same rank, such as 9 9 9 9.

Four Straight - A poker hand of four cards in sequence, not of the same suit, such as 3♥ 4♣ 5♠ 6♣. This is called an open ended straight, since there are two ways to improve it to a straight, either by drawing a 2 or a 7.

Full House - A poker hand that consists of a pair plus three of a kind, such as 8 8 J J J.

Gutshot Straight - A poker hand that consists of four cards, needing an interior card to form a Straight, such as 8♣ 9♠ J♥ Q♥. It is much more difficult to make a straight with this hand, needing the 10, and the odds against are approximately 11-1.

High Card - A jack, queen, king or ace, which, if paired in certain video poker games, will pay back the original bet to the player.

Hold Button - A button that, if pressed, will hold a particular card in the original hand, so that it will not be replaced by the draw. A hold button is under each card shown on the screen for that purpose.

Jokers Wild - A form of video poker that has a joker in addition to the regular 52 card deck. The joker is used as a wild card to improve or make any poker hand. For example, 3♠ 6♠ 10♠ J♠ Joker, makes this hand a flush.

Kicker - An odd card, which is usually a high card, held by the player prior to the draw. An example might be an Ace held with a pair of threes. Though this tactic may be useful in regular poker, it is not recommended in Video Poker.

Low Pair - A pair of 10s or lower ranked pair, which doesn't qualify for a payout in the game of Jacks or Better Video Poker.

Mechanic - The casino employee who repairs any machine that is broken.

Original Hand - The first five cards dealt to a player before he draws cards to improve the hand.

Progressive Machines - Video poker machines whose highest payout for a Royal Flush is not fixed, but increases each time a player inserts coins and doesn't get the Royal flush. Progressive machines usually start at 4,000 coins and move up from there till a Royal Flush is hit.

Royal Flush - The best hand in poker consisting of the Ace, King, Queen, Jack and 10 of the same suit. This hand qualifies for the biggest payout in Video Poker.

Straight - Five cards in consecutive sequence, but not of the same suit, such as 7♦ 8♦ 9♦ 10♣ J♣. A straight can also consist of Ace 2 3 4 and 5, as well as 10 J Q K A not of the same suit.

Straight Flush - Five cards in sequence and of the same suit but without an ace, such as 9♦ 10♦ J♦ Q♦ K♦. This is the second strongest hand in Video Poker.

Three of a Kind - A hand consisting of three cards of the same rank, such as 4 4 4 together with two odd cards.

Three to a Royal - A poker hand in which three cards necessary to form a Royal Flush are present, without the other two cards. An example might be 10♣ J♣ A♣.

Two Pair - A hand containing two separate pairs, such as K K 5 5, together with an odd card.

Well - The area in the bottom of the machine to which paid out coins fall.

GREAT HANDHELD CASINO GAMES!

By Radica - Featuring their Best Handheld Units!

From Radica's high-end Monte Carlo series, we've selected these ergonomic and stylish games to keep you in the fun. These **exciting palm-sized** games fit into your pockets and can be taken anywhere! Get ready for lots of fun and challenges. They're **easy-to-use**; even better, one or two can play. Large LCD screens bring the excitement of Las Vegas to you! Advance game functions, streamline designs with lids, tactile rubber keypads, music and red winner light. (Requires 2 AAA batteries.)

2-in-1 Slot Combo - $39.95

Regular Las Vegas style casino slots and European style nudge slots is the closest thing to playing for real. Features 1-5 lines of betting and good action in a sleek design.

3-in-1 Video Poker Combo - $39.95

Three games in one! Draw poker, deuces poker and loball poker (low hands are winners!). Random shuffling and payout schedules keeps the game realistic. Hours of fun!

2-in-1 Blackjack Combo - $39.95

Regular single deck 21 with all features - double down, hit, stand, split, insurance, surrender; *and* face-up blackjack - see dealer's cards! Deck automatically shuffles when low or you press button.

60

HIGH-LOW-SPLIT FOR ADVANCED PLAYERS *Ray Zee*. Advice from top pro on 7 stud & Omaha 8-or-Better; two books in one. Details tons of concepts; starting hands, disguising play, position, bluffing, high/low hand play, scare cards, end play, analyzing opponents, raise strategy, increasing wins, much more. 333 pgs, $34.95.

TOURNAMENT POKER *by Tom McEvoy*. Rated by pros as best book on tournaments ever written, and enthusiastically endorsed by 5 world champions -*a must for every player's library.* Packed solid with winning strategies for all 11 games in the *World Series of Poker*. Covers 7-card stud, limit hold'em, pot-limit hold'em, no-limit hold'em, Omaha high-low. Also, re-buy tournaments, satellites, half/half tourneys, strategies for each stage of play, profiles on big player lifestyles. 344 pages, $39.95

OMAHA HI-LO POKER *by Shane Smith*. Learn essential strategies for beating Omaha high-low; the best starting hands, how to play the flop, turn, and river, reading the board, dangerous draws, plus powerful chapter on winning low-limit tournaments. Learn the differences between Omaha high-low and hold'em strategies. Includes odds charts, glossary, low-limit tips. 84 pages, 8 x 11, $17.95

7-STUD (COMPLETE COURSE IN WINNING AT MEDIUM & LOWER LIMITS) *By Roy West*. Learn the latest strategies for winning at $1-$4 spread-limit up to $10-$20 fixed-limit games. Covers starting hands, 3rd-7th street strategy for playing most hands, overcards, selective aggressiveness, reading hands, secrets of the pros, psychology, more - in a 42 "lesson" informal format. Includes bonus chapter on 7-stud tournament strategy by World Champion Tom McEvoy. 160 pages, $24.95.

AVERY CARDOZA'S CASINO

THE COMPLETE CASINO EXPERIENCE & PROFESSIONAL GAMBNLING TUTOR

For CD-ROM Windows 3.1 & 95 - Requires 486 or better, 8MB RAM

65 GAME VARIETIES - SIX MAJOR GAMES!

GET READY FOR A GREAT TIME! Enter Avery Cardoza's incredible 3D casino world where *you're really part of the action.* 65 great game varieties include 1, 2, 4 and 6 deck blackjack, 40 different slots, double odds craps - all options, 17 video poker machines, big action roulette and virtual keno!

REAL INTERACTION! This is the *only* game where you have complete interaction: choose any of 4 ways to roll the dice *and* how long to roll 'em in craps; play up to 3 hands in blackjack; go for a royal flush, pull for a jackpot, make over 150 roulette bets, play keno with a 100,000 game history! Dealers are also part of the action! With responses tied to 257 criteria, you never know what they'll say or do!

STATE-OF-THE-ART GRAPHICS! It took one million dollars to create 10,577 hand enhanced 3D animation frames, digital voice/effects, full animations!

HAVE FUN & LEARN TO BE A WINNER!

EXPERT ON-LINE TUTORIAL AND STATS! Learn the best play for *every* situation; how to play a 16 vs. 10, turn hot craps rolls into monster wins, find slots & video poker machines ripe for jackpots, more! Use *Ask the Expert* to analyze every move, the Coach to alert on bad plays,or go solo! Also, 577 fields track every vital stat. Want to know how many 21's, full houses or jackpots you got, percentage of correct winning plays, most money you made, biggest craps shoot? It's all here.

FREE BONUS BOOK! ($15.00 VALUE) - Includes free 176 page professional strategy guide from gambling guru Avery Cardoza with tips for all the games.